MW01244681

FOR HER NAME'S SAKE

Created by the publishing team of Beyond the Book Media

Cover design

The scriptural quotations in this book are from The New Oxford
Annotated Bible, Third Edition. Oxford University Press: New York.
New Revised Standard Version Bible, copyright © 1989 the Division
of Christian Education of the National Council of the Churches of
Christ in the United States of America.

Photographer: Cara Lynn Birts Photography

Copyright 2020 by **Monica M. Leak**. All rights reserved. No part
of this book may be reproduced by any means without the written
permission of the publisher, Beyond the Book Media,

Printed in the United States of America

ISBN-978-1-953788-18-4

MONICA LEAK

FOR HER NAME'S SAKE

Dedication

This collection of poetry is dedicated to the women whose lives were disrupted due to police brutality. Some of these may be names you have heard through news and media outlets, while others may be unknown. Yet each one deserves to have their stories told and their lives to be remembered

Preface

Born on a Friday
On time for Bible study
Preacher's kid all day
Under strict rule my life would be
But it was in creative writing that I would discover my identity
Had the tools and blessing of my faith
Stories and poems in journals that wouldn't see the light of day
Police brutality took over the news with a sense of urgency of now
The church should be saying or doing something, someway,
somehow
But as a woman in the church, too often, we're told to be silent
As if cooking or teaching children is the sole purpose of God for
our lives
So I couldn't sit idly by
Just watching videos of sisters and brothers fighting for their lives
So under the unction of the Spirit that stirred my creative side
I began to say their names, and their stories began to write
Some of these names may be familiar because you heard them on
the news
Yet others' lives were just as valued, and their voices deserved to be
lifted too
So the telling takes the form of the order of worship in a
traditional church
I took the concept and let it flow for all its worth
Saying their names and uplifting their stories is a reminder that
freedom ain't really free
It comes at a high cost, and we must continue to speak truth to
power
Just for the right to live and breathe
The call of Micah 6:8 to love mercy, do justly, and walk humbly
with God is yet the cause
This is my why, to call us to the remembrance of this word
To say the names and tell the stories until we see freedom and
justice for all.

TABLE OF CONTENTS

PROCESSIONAL

We gather as sisters into this sacred space
We come to pray, sing, bare our all on the altar of the Holy place
We assemble as one in body, mind, and spirit
To claim our identity of creation in the Divine image
Not to be treated with violence and cruelty to be savagely ravaged
Let the congregation rise and receive declaration and proclamation
As women of all races, creeds, ethnicities, and classes enter into formation

HANDLE WITH CARE

We are so strong
Matriarch
Always angry
Promiscuous
Welfare queen
Neglectful
Bad mother
Smaller brained
The tropes of the black woman

But the reality
The reality of the capacity of the mind
Knowledge
To be soft
To be feminine
To speak one's mind
To hold her own
To voice what needs and should be heard

We deserve that
We are owed that
A debt long overdue
Like we can't be overwhelmed
Like we can't suffer anxiety
Like we can't feel or lose control
Without being deemed crazy
Any show of this returns us to failure
A failure to live up to society's image

So, when we have a mental meltdown
When we need help
We call on those from whom we can get knowledgeable support
Yet you sent officers with only the skill to restrain
What was to be an escort to a hospital to get a psychiatric eval
Turns into a news story that we all know too well

Amid an escort struggle, the body becomes limp
The cops applied excessive use of force
To restrain another life lost in death
Wrestled to the ground with a knee to the back
What kind of trained response to a mental health crisis is any of that?

I am a black woman
Strong in mind, body, and spirit
Reflection of the Divine image
Beautiful
With integrity in my dealings
Brave
Sometimes scared
Sometimes afraid
Bold
Black women
If all things were equal and fair
They'd learn some respect and handle with care

#Tanisha Anderson

HOW TO BREAK UP A FIGHT

Assess the situation
Parties involved
Assess surroundings
Residential
Business
Parking lot
Hiding places
Secure spaces
Self-assess
Keep your distance
Place your own safety first

You got this?
Or do you need backup?
Your crew got your back?
Or are they quick to dodge and jet?
Better self-assess
Use nonviolent means
Ask a question
What is the underlying cause?
Get to the root of a thing

Don't jump to conclusions based on appearances
'Cause that's how folks wind up hurt
Just jumping in the mix with no clue of what it is
Understand the relationships
Examine the motivation
What was going on wasn't under your investigation?

You were on scene for another situation

A and B conversation, so what are you here for?
Then want to confront and demand the dropping of a supposed gun
Hello, it's a cell phone in the car
For a video, it's a prop, a fake gun replica
Duh just duh
Seriously an officer of the law can't tell fake from the real
Requirements must be at an all-time low if no one has that skill

You inserted yourself into the situation
Accusing me of making a threatening motion
None of that happened here

No distance
No use of nonviolence
No self-assessment
No assessment of the situation
No understanding of the persons involved
No asking or answering questions
Just an automatic response to a supposed threat to pop
And with shots in the back pop off

No determining of the facts
No taking stock of self before taking aim
No empathy
No conversation
Officers only placed on administrative leave
Further investigation pending
Go figure

The situation?
Aspiring rapper
Engaged
Accepting girlfriend's kids as his own
Having an argument
Not your concern
Just busybodies
Asserting "authority"
Time to retake
How to Break Up a Fight

#India Beaty

CALL TO WORSHIP

Leader: In this time of the pandemic, we as women have experienced joy and loss

People: Sisters have gathered today with bowed heads and heavy hearts

Leader: The Lord, who hears our prayers and supplications, will offer you abiding and healing love and peace.

People: Thanks be to God for extending favor, continued strength, and grace.

Leader: Let your hearts not be weary in the work of justice but empowered with the strength of the Spirit to be the change and hearts opened to receive God's everlasting mercy

People: Our spirits are opened to receive God's abiding love for us.

Everyone: AMEN.

I'M NOT LEAVING

I'm not leaving
I'm not leaving
What are you looking at?
Call the police? No need for that
Just trying to get treated like anyone else
Been suffering from some pain
Trying to take care of myself
Going to emergency rooms one, two, now three
Young, black, and homeless
Is that why they won't treat me?
With all the dollars and cents invested in healthcare
The ones in need can't even get seen, and that's not even fair

I'm not leaving
I'm not leaving
I live out in the elements
Sometimes in the cold, sometimes in the rain
I came here for treatment 'cause I'm experiencing some leg pain
I'm in a wheelchair dropped by officers to the ground
Where is the humanity in the arresting act?
None to be found
Why are you just standing there?
How do you expect me to get out of the car without my wheelchair?
Then to be carried into a jail cell and placed on the floor
I'm a living, breathing being, not some wild animal.

So, I would leave the hospital
Without the treatment for the pain that I'd come for

Blood clot in legs untreated soon move to lungs and ends all pain
How do you die in police custody?
Being young, homeless, black, and refusing to leave

#Anna Brown

I FORGOT MY MEDS

'Cause I didn't take my meds
911 was called
Just a little off, a little something in my head
Playing some music to make me feel better
Just closed off in my room to get myself together

But because I didn't take my meds
911 was called
You didn't send just an ambulance
Because of a report of a knife, you brought the police
You send the inept to address a schizophrenic's needs

They barged into the house like a scene from a movie
I had a knife for the sake of protecting me
Knocked down the door like a full attack
How did they expect anybody to act?

So, with a knife in hand
I take a lunge, scarring an officer and stabbing one
Did they take any time to de-escalate the situation?
Not even. None
Shots fired, situation done

Excuses are made for the loss of life
The man just called for help and said
You didn't have to shoot my wife
Police meant to serve and protect, not to harm
According to their recall of things, they attempted to disarm

Yet instead claimed they tried to reason with a person who is knowingly mentally ill
They aren't equipped for that kind of service
They don't have the knowledge or the skill
Just a shame that it seems to always end this way
Police can snuff out a life and make a clean getaway

#Martina Brown

DOXOLOGY

Praise God in whom freedom and justice lives
Praise God all receivers of forgiveness
Praise boldly before the Holy throne
Praise be to the Anointed One

Amen

FOR BEING LATE

Got the arthritis
Got a touch of sugar
Doing the best I can
Living check to check
Just to keep food on the table
Just to keep clothes on my back
Just to keep a roof over my head
At $89.44 a month
I need some help
Just a little behind
Ain't got many options

Not sure what will happen
Daughter says not to open the doors
No strangers
What's going on?
What did I do?
Footsteps
Pounding
In the kitchen
Grab a butcher knife
Scared
Find a place
Naked
Closet-sized safe space

SWAT team
6 officers

Bulletproof vests
Shotguns
Shields surrounding
Restraining prods
Lunge to defend
Shot in the hand
Not enough to disarm

Even with apology
Still shot in the chest
For late payment
For mental illness
For being a senior citizen
For being poor
For being black
For being a woman
For being 300 pounds of intimidation
For being a threat
For being late

1,2,3,4,5 months late
Always been late
No questions why late
No intervention for being late
No, how may we help you 'cause you're late
Just section 8, and we can't wait
No convictions, and as always, the murderers escape
No matter the policies, the procedures that you know put in place
No one should have to die for a payment being late

#Eleanor Bumpers

GOT BAIL?

Needed help
Emergency help
In a mental crisis help
Can you send some help?
Help
Please, help

Got bail?
Yeah bail
That state of release
That money given
Ensure one in custody returns
Returns on the appointed date
Returns at the appointed time
Yeah bail
That bail
Got bail?

The response to a mental health call
Transfer to a holding center
Arraignment and bail set at 15K
Who you know got that lying around?
Cost more than a piece of car without the bells and whistles
That's college tuition for a semester
Because of disorderly conduct
No priors
Got bail?

Everything didn't get reported
At least by those in charge
To leave out these kinds of details
Just seems strange and a little odd
The stories of what really happened
Wouldn't come until afterward

See, you get the call
They running out of the house
Flagging for help
Alleged punching of the motorist
To take off in the car
Two vehicles and then a school bus hit
Refused to get out of the car
A scuffle
To be described as combative
Told police about smoking something

No hospital visitation
No toxicology screening
Just straight to court
To be charged with a list of new criminal offenses
Another case of pin the blame on the victim in this nonsense

Who got it?
How can a poor, young black girl get it?
Why it got to be so high?
So, is this why mistreatment is justified?
17 days in custody
Without proper medical attention

Pulmonary embolism suffered
Result of renal failure
Dehydration
Rhabdomyolysis
And a broken arm
An arm broken, possibly during the arrest
Bail should have been set for the deputies in this mess
Anybody got bail?

This wasn't the help
Not the requested help
Not the mental help
The help called for
The response needed
Where was the bail?

Got bailout for big corporations
Bailouts for the rich
Bail so easy if you've got it on the ready
Bail ain't got no payment plan
If you ain't got it
You ain't got it
You get stuck without recourse
Suffering consequences of no wrong done

Nothing wrong
Just young
Just poor
Just black
Just a woman
With mental health concerns

Without options
Without resources
To be held in custody

To be found
Naked without clothing
Without undergarments
Without water
Without a blanket
No access to a shower
Not even a mattress

Can you get me out?
Just get me out
I need out
I want out
Bail me out

Not even a mental health exam
The purpose of the 911 call
Nobody thought to follow through on that
Nobody thought of it at all
Broken arm not even treated
Antipsychotic meds prescribed
Nobody ensuring it was properly taken

Physical condition declining
Mental health condition worsening
Lying on the floor
Probably still covered in urine and feces
Can't get out

Will I make it out?

You watched this
17 days of mental and physical decline
The interview with a mental health counselor report was shoddy at
best
Didn't result in a psych referral
Can't you see evidence of incompetence and neglect?

Officers watched this
Knew the conditions
Day after day
Supposedly following protocol
Policies they had in place

This is the help
The kind of help
They give to the ill and the poor
To rob folks blind of a high set bail
To be incarcerated and inhumanely lie on the floor
In the end to say they were happy about the care given
If there had been care, wouldn't somebody still be living?

Needed help
Emergency help
Mental crises help
Only asked for help
Death in custody was not the help

#India Cummings

INVOCATION

We enter to Your presence, Creator of heaven and earth
To bring before You our worship and praise
For You alone are worthy
We acknowledge and repent of our wrong
But ask that You look down upon our collective pain
See your children yet in cages
See your children divided by structural racism
See your children divided over politics and policies
Open our hearts that we will feel
Open our minds to understanding
Open our eyes to see the reality of what's happening around us
Open our ears to actively listen to the joys and pains of others
Open our spirits to connect
To connect heart to heart
That we come to know what it is to be our brother's keeper
That we come to know what it is to be our sister's keeper
That we know what it is to be a good neighbor
That we will lead peaceful lives in love, honor, and honesty

Amen

A BAD COMBINATION

Sometimes you just have a taste for something sweet
No rhyme nor reason
Just satisfying a want and need
Bubble gum, jolly ranchers, sugar daddies, or candy bars
Something sweet to eat
That's what the candy is for

And every now and then, you just want a little taste
Something that goes down nice and smooth
Not letting a drop go to waste
Ain't nothing new, a habit for years
I know the consequences
No need for you to interfere
With my plan of self-care, a couple of beers

Candy and beer
Arrested for an outstanding warrant
Over some candy and beer
Get arrested at the hospital
$1,150 in fines for some candy and beer
Bench warrant served in a hospital
Four years later over candy and beer
Already checked in at the emergency room

If son was so concerned, then what reason
What reason for a son to call 911?
Already in the place where she was going to receive help
Rather her to go to jail than having to bury her

Didn't realize that attempts to help would result in her death
See, these officers don't hear the cries of a black woman's pain
We're only faking and attention-seeking; that's their claim

Yes, an issue of alcoholism the family was concerned
Intervention gone wrong; death in police custody
Makes no sense that a life is lost
A bad combination of candy and beer

#Joyce Curnell

ENDANGERED

400 years of slavery
Reconstruction
And Jim Crow
Fight for Civil Rights, and justice yet goes on
Yet nothing is more endangered than the life of a black woman

Just like an animal being hunted down
Slaves and mammies
Domestics to entrepreneurs
Child bearers and caregivers
We undergird the very foundation
Burden bearers without protection
Endangered, the black woman

Equal protection under the law
Repeats like a broken record
Reverberating like the blow of a curse word
Voices and pleas for help get silenced
Silenced at every turn
Life under fire, the endangered black woman

Quick to be falsely accused
Pregnant yet suffering violence for alleged drug transaction and use
Arrested and placed in a police car after a resistant scuffle
Witnesses say these allegations are untrue
There was no scuffle or transaction
Yet the victim becomes prey when another claim is made
That she was shot in the head when in officer's unmarked car she

tried to get away

How's she going to drive sitting in the back of a squad car?
Is this just bad reporting, or is just speaking the truth too hard?
How much longer can this disrespect for life go on?
Waking up daily to find whose name has been added
To the list of the endangered black woman

A 31-year-old pregnant black woman
Dead by a policeman's gunshot to the neck
So protests erupt in the streets, demanding justice
That's all we want to get
But our shouts and cries continue to fall on deaf ears
To be next on the endangered list becomes every black woman's fear

#Danette Daniels

HYMN OF PRAISE (PSALMS 103:1-5, NRSV)

Bless the Lord, O my soul, and all that is within me,
bless his holy name.
Bless the Lord, O my soul, and do not forget all his benefits—
who forgives all your iniquity, who heals all your diseases,
who redeems your life from the Pit, who crowns you with steadfast
love and mercy,
who satisfies you with good as long as you live so that your youth is
renewed like the eagle's.

ON THE RESERVATION

On the reservation
We are tribe
We are tradition
We are one with nature
We are one with spirit
We are connected one to the other
You don't come in unless invited
Only to leave
For the basics we need
On the reservation

We are Muckleshoot
Descendants of the Duwamish and Upper Puyallup peoples
We are federally recognized
In the area of Western Washington state
We call our sacred home
Linked by ties of marriage
Ceremony
Commerce
Land
We forged a quality of life on our own
We are Muckleshoot
On this our reservation

On the reservation
Young daughter, young sister
In a season of life and love
Connected to her people

Connected to the land
Maturing in the native ways
The bounty and resources we have

Yet off the reservation
Near pow-wow grounds
A boyfriend makes a request of a deputy
Out of love and concern
To check on his woman, his girl
Having made threats and thoughts of suicide
He was seeking help
From the resources he knew
Off the reservation
Maybe they could come through

At the request of the boyfriend, deputies come onto the reservation
No preplanning done or notes taken
A preparatory investigation
Officers arrive unprepared for a woman in a mental crisis situation
Like some TV crime series
Officers pound, knock down and kick in her bedroom door
With children ages 2 and 3 standing around in the hall

Davis was lying in the bed
They claim she pointed a gun at them
Officers then fired 8 rounds into her
Not knowing she was 4 months pregnant
Seems like they should have been able
To disarm a woman lying in her bed
But natural instincts and adrenaline kicks in
And they fill the air with the sound of blasting lead

Gun was unloaded, and it seems there was tampering with evidence
Prior to others' arrival
It's funny how much effort is made to get a story straight
Rather than for a woman writhing in blood on the floor for survival

Were there no healers to speak life and sound mind without fear and trepidation?
Bringing outsiders to infect our land from the reservation
A community torn and bound together with a shared grief
Seek answers, seeking justice for relief
On the reservation

#Renee Davis

WHO'S TO BLAME

Got things to do
Places to go
People to see
I'm trying to hit every green light
Just move out the way
Let me through

Call it reckless
Call it erratic
I'm trying to get somewhere
Just a little crash
Of course, here comes Mr. Officer
To pull me aside
Ain't nobody got time for this foolishness

Got things to do
Places to go
People to see
Just leave me be

Passenger door opened
One down
Gonna reverse it
Another one tries to get it in with arms in the car
Pull off and back
Shot fired into chest
Claims accident

Nothing will get done
Going interrupted
People will be waiting
What have I got myself in?

Car crashes
Get out of the car
Staggering
Stumbling
Blood soaked
Fall
Taken to the hospital
Just to go into cardiac arrest
Shortly after arrival to be pronounced dead

Accidental discharge is what the police will claim
Too bad witnesses don't see it the same
At the end of the day, who's to blame?

#Shantel Davis

RESPONSIVE READING

Leader: Exodus 9:1,2, 7b (NRSV) Then the Lord said to Moses, "Go to Pharaoh, and say to him, 'Thus says the Lord, the God of the Hebrews: Let my people go, so that they may worship me. 2 For if you refuse to let them go and still hold them, 7b. But the heart of Pharaoh was hardened, and he would not let the people go.

People: I will be prepared for resistance. I will use this time to learn and teach others the way.

Leader: Exodus 9:27-28 (NRSV) 27 Then Pharaoh summoned Moses and Aaron, and said to them, "This time I have sinned; the Lord is in the right, and I and my people are in the wrong. 28 Pray to the Lord! Enough of God's thunder and hail! I will let you go; you need stay no longer."

People: I acknowledge my mistakes and faults. My decisions and choices have not always been the best yet holding on to them does not better the present. I choose now to do that which is right and will contribute to the highest good.

Leader: Exodus 9:34-35 (NRSV) "34 But when Pharaoh saw that the rain and the hail and the thunder had ceased, he sinned once more and hardened his heart, he and his officials. 35 So the heart of Pharaoh was hardened, and he would not let the Israelites go, just as the Lord had spoken through Moses."

People: When I arrive on the other side of a situation, I'll remember that the letting go of that which I do not need will heal and bring wholeness.

Leader: Exodus 11:1 (NRSV) "The Lord said to Moses, "I will bring one more plague upon Pharaoh and upon Egypt; afterwards he will let you go from here; indeed, when he lets you go, he will drive you away."

All: I know that freedom means letting go of things that do not serve, respect, honor and protect me, my family, my neighbor, and larger community. I will not hold on to false narratives, rhetoric, and single accounts to be the basis of my beliefs about others. As a member of the beloved community, I hold to faith, hope, and love and release the hate that I do not need.

IF I'M IN YOUR CARE

If I'm in your care
The responsibility for my well-being is yours
The basics of daily living
These are the things that should be provided
Food, clothing, shelter
Basics just basics
If I'm in your care

Whether privately owned or tax-funded
Places of incarceration, custody, or holding
They are yet responsible for care
You can't point fingers and shift blame
Especially when video evidence is there

Too often, the victim is turned criminal
By a dig into the past
Ignore the situation at current
Rather than bringing those in charge to task
Let's bring past mistakes to the forefront
All those little details which to the present case are irrelevant

New environment
Feeling isolated
You find ways to cope
Grieving loss of a brother
I made a choice
I took my pain meds
I wanted to feel numb

Excessive drinking would cause me to become undone

An arrest by campus police shifted the power and control
Trying to advocate for self
Worse than a child hearing
Just do what you're told
Having problems breathing
Asked for some air
Taken to the rec yard
Asked for some water
See the video taken by a bystander's cell
Without physical assistance
Less than 2 hours later, found dead
While I'm in your care

Bruises and contusions
A lacerated lip appears
If this had been a child
Somebody would be calling the welfare

Bruises on the upper and lower torso
And bruises on face and other body parts left unexplained
A mother in grief trying get to the source
Refusal to provide autopsy pictures and video footage
Department of Justice now her only recourse

To be without answers speaks as something wrong there
If a living, breathing human dies in your care

#Ahjah Dixon

CHOICES

Each day is full of choices
You wake up in the morning
You choose to get up
Or hit the snooze for 5 more minutes
You get up and make a choice
Quick wash or full shower
You choose what to wear
Power suit or business casual
You make a choice
Just coffee or full-scaled breakfast
Choices
Morning choices

To comb or not comb your hair
Deodorant or go all natural
To brush and floss your teeth
To shave or not to shave
To iron or to steam
Lotion or baby oil
To pack a lunch
Pick up something in route
Drive or carpool
In-office or telework
Choices
Daily Choices

But over life and death?
You have no choice?

Absolutely these five officers had no other choice
The woman was under suspicion for a stolen vehicle
Upon stopping and getting out of the vehicle
She had a gun, of course
Wouldn't you feel threatened for your life?
She was totally outnumbered and outgunned
Couldn't she have been taken down without having to die?
Life and death choices

Reasonable and lawful according to the district attorney's report
This is how the officers' choice is described
As usual, they were in fear for their very lives
Why the need to shoot multiple times?
Even if in the wrong, why play God and take a life?
Witnesses say the officers asked her
To surrender several times and she'd go unharmed
It was a 40-minute standoff when she pulled that gun
And the choice was made without delay
Another black woman would die today

Because of choices
Response choices
Dangerous choices
Life and death choices
Can't say you had no choices
You just chose differently
Choices

#Sharmel Edwards

AFFIRMATION OF FAITH

"We believe in God the Almighty who hovered in love over the primeval chaos and uttered creation into existence out of a holy mess.

We believe in the One who breathed the breath of life into human and engendered the primal family and community into being

We believe in the magnificent signature of God's image in every human being, signed in infinite variety, and sewn in multicolored splendor, even when it is humanly difficult to experience it in our damaged bodies.

We believe in the self-revelatory signature of God in Jesus Christ who came to restore healing and wholeness into every fiber of our existence.

We believe in Jesus Christ who came to show that salvation is healing and wholeness, and who opened our eyes that we may see each other into God's image– beyond the troubling stereotyping and systemic use of race, ethnicity, class, sexuality, disability, and other identity markers to divide and fragment us.

We believe in Jesus who came to open our hearts to the God who so-loved-the- world, and who calls forth discipleship from among us to the alleviation of human suffering. That we may see the whole world of ours, as never before, as a God-loved, God-breathed, and God-reconciled world.

We believe in the Crucified God who embraces with his wounded arms those who die alone at this time.

We believe in the Resurrected Savior who invites us to touch his wounds, if we lack belief during these times of paralyzing fear and numbing trauma.

We believe in the Holy Spirit who fosters connected relationships across the divides, while we sit with ourselves.

We believe in the Holy Spirit who always pushes the church to reach out to the margins and enter into the exilic homes through the gifts of technology, nudging each of us to birth hope and resilience. We, also, believe that the digital divide is human-created and greed-sponsored, and the front-line workers embody flesh-and-blood communication.

We believe that beyond the ravages of time and this pandemic, we will be restored into wellness and wholeness, with different understandings of what it is to be the Church in the world.

We believe that one day, we will be fully restored into God's image and God's healed Body. Then wholeness will be the theme of the great orchestral music of the Church and the cosmos.

Until then, we will build bridges of healing and reconciliation with each other and God's creation.

Therefore, we will commit ourselves every day to healing and wholeness until that day. Amen." [1]

1. Dharmaraj, Glory E. Affirmation of Faith. https://nationalcouncilofchurches.us/an-affirmation-of-faith/ Posted April 27, 2020. Accessed 9/27/20

IF THIS IS THE KIND OF HELP

If this is the kind of help you're giving, I...
Missed a counseling session because of a storm
Got a diagnosis for which I'm being treated
Mood disorder and depression
Had already been hospitalized once
For cutting myself

If this is the kind of help you're giving, I....
Just made a call
A call to get some help
I felt myself spiraling into the darkness
What gets sent is not social services
Or a mental health provider or even an ambulance
I get a cop, a trigger-happy policeman

If this is the kind of help you're giving, I...
Can get off the couch
Hands raised and empty
Shots fired

If this is the kind of help you're giving, I...
Guess the call was made
For being taken to a mental health facility
You have everyone down so you can change the scene
Set up your story
Nah, man, that ain't gonna fly

If this is the kind of help you're giving, I...
Don't want it.
I don't need it.
Don't even offer it.

'Cause your help ain't help at all

If this is the kind of help you're giving

#Janisha Fonville

WHO'LL BE A WITNESS?

Who'll be a witness?
A witness who can say what they saw
A witness who can tell what they heard
A witness who can describe the scene and circumstances

Who'll be a witness?
A witness that can verify
Who answers in truth, not reported lies?
Who can say from a witness stand
It was a cell phone, not a gun in her hands?

Who'll be a witness?
Who saw what happened at this traffic stop?
Was the victim in the car, or did she get out with her hands up?
Was it a gun, a cell phone in hand, or a silver padlock?
Can I get a witness?

Officers, always quick to say they feared for their lives
But the silver padlock "gun"
Was on the floor on the passenger's side
Right hand vs. left on hand
It was a cell phone
Can I get a witness?

Can I get a witness?
Yeah
Just one more witness?
Yeah

A good-hearted witness?
Yeah
Will you be a witness?
Yeah

Let the witness speak for truth
Let the witness speak for what is right
Let the witness stand up and tell it like it happened
Will there be one?

#LaTonya Haggerty

ANTHEM: LIFT EV'RY VOICE AND SING

WRITTEN AND COMPOSED BY JAMES WELDON JOHNSON

"Lift ev'ry voice and sing, till earth and heaven ring,
Ring with the harmonies of liberty;
Let our rejoicing rise, high as the list'ning skies,
Let it resound loud as the rolling sea.
Sing a song full of the faith that the dark past has taught us,
Sing a song full of the hope that the present has brought us;
Facing the rising sun of our new day begun,
Let us march on till victory is won.

Stony the road we trod, bitter the chastening rod,
Felt in the days when hope unborn had died;
Yet with a steady beat, have not our weary feet,
Come to the place for which our fathers sighed?
We have come over a way that with tears has been watered,
We have come, treading our path through the blood of the
slaughtered;
Out from the gloomy past, till now we stand at last
Where the white gleam of our bright star is cast.

God of our weary years, God of our silent tears,
Thou who hast brought us thus far on the way;
Thou who hast by Thy might, led us into the light,
Keep us forever in the path, we pray.
Lest our feet stray from the places, our God, where we met Thee.
Lest our hearts, drunk with the wine of the world, we forget Thee.
Shadowed beneath Thy hand, may we forever stand,
True to our God, true to our native land."

ONLY 17

I'm seventeen
Just seventeen
Puberty? Totally over it
Hormones kicking in
Got my cycle
Ugh, cramps….HELLO!
Glad that acne cleared up
I'm seventeen

I am responsible
Making some decisions
I've got options
College or workforce
Becoming focused
Setting some goals
I'm seventeen

Independence in motion
Can I get some space, please?
Making deep connections
Crew is solid
Friends for life
Heartache, Heartbreak, or oh so in love
Don't try me
Gotta love me
I'm seventeen

Still taking risks
Maybe somewhat fewer
Don't know it all
Going to make some mistakes, many or few
Making commitments
Keeping commitments
Taking on more roles
Looking for intimacy
I'm seventeen

I have my own way of speaking
Got ways of dealing with stuff better than as a kid
I'm nearly grown
Got my license
Trying to spread my wings
I'm seventeen

Accidents happen
I hit the front of a police car
Put the car in reverse
Hit a parked car
Drove forward through a ditch
Kinda hit a bystander
Before hitting another parked car
Only to get shot by an officer
To die of my injuries
Seventeen just seventeen

Hopes, dreams, ambitions?
Died
Prom and graduation?

Not happening
No college or career
No marriage, no kids
No making my claim in the world

Not a dream deferred
Not a promise denied
Gone in an instant
A split decision
'Cause disabling a vehicle was not an option
Just automatic shoot to kill
Only seventeen

Investigations unending
Leading to no answers
Wanting community to remain calm
Sounding like Slick Rick's, Children's Story
Just another black girl whose world came crashing

Crashing down
Ending in murder
Unresolved
Only seventeen

#Darnesha Harris

IDENTIFY

We identify a thing through our senses
Through sight, sound, smell, taste, or touch
We identify things through environment
Rural, inner-city, suburb
Hustle and bustle or small-town vibe

We identify through connections
Family, friends, classmates, work colleagues
And those with more intimate meaning
Yet everything can't be identified that easily
We may laugh until we cry but not because we're sad
We may scream to gain attention but not because we're scared
Everything can't easily be identified by sight
We don't always have the right identifiers at our hands or in our
sight

Unable to get a job, drug treatment, or find a shelter
One would or could easily identify this person as a nobody, a reject,
a loser
Yet there was more to her than outward appearances could see
She was transgender and fighting every day for the respect of her
identity
Just for walking down the street one night
Profiled and arrested by the cops on sight

Accused of prostitution though no contact was found
Slurs of "faggot" and "he-she" proceeded from officers' mouths
Choosing to take the high road and not respond to the officers' slurs

Duana was handcuffed, pepper-sprayed, and beaten face and head to the ground
Officers unaware that security footage captured every image and every sound
The main officer in this case would be federally prosecuted

An overhaul of the police department's sensitivity training began to be instituted
But not long after, Duana would be found shot execution-style
Violence for the way she self-identified
Her very being vilified

It's easy to pass over the story and say this is not my issue
Because of our ways of identifying, we fail to acknowledge the abuse
Equal justice under the law is what's at stake
For how one identifies is no one's right to take
Just something to think about and realize
No matter how you identify that bullet could be you next time

#Duana Johnson

SCRIPTURE LESSON

Old Testament Reading
Isaiah 25:1-9

O LORD, you are my God; I will exalt you, I will praise your name; for you have done wonderful things, plans formed of old, faithful and sure.
2 For you have made the city a heap, the fortified city a ruin; the palace of aliens is a city no more, it will never be rebuilt. 3 Therefore strong peoples will glorify you; cities of ruthless nations will fear you. 4 For you have been a refuge to the poor, a refuge to the needy in their distress, a shelter from the rainstorm and a shade from the heat.

When the blast of the ruthless was like a winter rainstorm, 5 the noise of aliens like heat in a dry place, you subdued the heat with the shade of clouds; the song of the ruthless was stilled.6 On this mountain the LORD of hosts will make for all peoples a feast of rich food, a feast of well-aged wines, of rich food filled with marrow, of well-aged wines strained clear. 7 And he will destroy on this mountain the shroud that is cast over all peoples, the sheet that is spread over all nations; 8 he will swallow up death forever.

Then the Lord GOD will wipe away the tears from all faces, and the disgrace of his people he will take away from all the earth, for the LORD has spoken.
9 It will be said on that day, Lo, this is our God; we have waited for him, so that he might save us. This is the LORD for whom we have waited; let us be glad and rejoice in his salvation.

Reading of Psalms
Psalms 25:1-9 (NRSV)

1 The LORD is my shepherd, I shall not want 2 He makes me lie down in green pastures;
he leads me beside still waters; 3 he restores my soul. He leads me in right paths for his name's sake.4 Even though I walk through the darkest valley, I fear no evil;
for you are with me; your rod and your staff—they comfort me.

5 You prepare a table before me in the presence of my enemies; you anoint my head with oil; my cup overflows.6 Surely goodness and mercy shall follow me all the days of my life, and I shall dwell in the house of the LORD my whole life long.

New Testament Reading

2 Corinthians 4:8-9 (NRSV), 8 We are afflicted in every way, but not crushed; perplexed, but not driven to despair; 9 persecuted, but not forsaken; struck down, but not destroyed.

THE NUMBERS

The numbers
Check the numbers
What are the numbers telling you?
CDC says 1 in 4 women
Then it says 1 in 7 men
Are not perpetrators of domestic violence
Not instigators of domestic violence
But will experience domestic violence
Like that look to the left and right in class
Then start counting to see whether you could be one
Or a few more numbers down the row could be one

Verbal Abuse
Physical Abuse
Emotional Abuse
Sexual Abuse
All wrapped up and tied up
Reflected in whole or part in cases of domestic violence

But what about the innocent?
What about the bystanders?
What about the family members who see what's going on?
What are the numbers?
Can you give me the numbers?
There have got to be numbers

Nah, the only number is the call made to state an emergency
A father calls for 911 to get help for his son

Police officers are sent to confront this domestic situation
The son is wielding and carrying a bat
How are the police going to handle that?

Ms. Bettie, a neighbor, was called to let the police into the home
No one could have counted the response
For doing that task, her life would be gone
Son comes out swinging, appearing combative
Officer's gun discharges
The son and the neighbor "accidentally" get killed

She just went to let the officers in
Not to become another black woman
Whose life comes to a tragic end
Doesn't matter if the city reached a settlement
This is just another epic fail in which nobody wins
The numbers
Another tragic number

#Bettie Jones

DON'T LET ME DIE

Life is a precious gift
Each moment, each breath
The senses embrace the height
Embrace the depth
Of all that is light
Of all that is life

Can we put a value on life?
Some say yes in their fight for the unborn
Allowing the cries of the living to be ignored
Yes, you value black celebrities on TV and magazine covers
While we are bombarded by videos of the deaths of one more sister
or brother
Yeah, we value our American freedoms but can't define what they are
Ask any child if they know the story behind the flag's stripes and
stars
We place value on the amassing of wealth or accomplishment of
degrees
But show no care or concern for those the Scripture calls the least
of these

The matter is life
Your life, my life, our lives
Can we live it?
Can we feel it?
Can we walk in it?
Can we see the truth revealed in it?
Knowing that in the cycle of being that our God-breathed life
mattered?

So even if in life some wrong I've done
That does not negate my being fully human
Human deserving of empathy
Human deserving of compassion
Human deserving of understanding
Simply Human
I know why I'm here
I know what got me here
I'm not fighting being here
Just don't let me die here

I know my health issues
I know my medical needs
Why can't you hear my cry?
Why don't you understand my pleas?
Deliver me from the hands of blue-uniformed enemies

My meds are prescribed
You have to follow the dosage, follow the times
You've got a log to keep record of that
Failing to follow standards, a department's slack
So, the needs of a black woman in pain can't be taken seriously
If you were going to give the wrong meds at all, you should have let it be
My times fell in the hands of those who held me in custody.

Don't
Don't let
Don't let me
Don't let me die
Don't let me die here

Didn't want to die here
Nobody deserves to die here
Didn't expect to die here
Didn't plan to die here
Succumbing to now a black body's greatest fear

#Ralkina Jones

PASTORAL PRAYER
(MATTHEW 21; PHILIPPIANS 2)

Gracious God our Creator,
Teach us Your ways
Help us to honor You in our words and deeds
We ask of You what is Your will for us this day?
Shall it be in acts of kindness to others, offering of praise to you,
Uplifted prayers and giving of gifts?
To whom will You call us to serve?
Help us to trust Your leading and direction.
Help us listen and adhere to Your still small voice.
We ask Your blessings upon this community of believers
As we gather in worship.
Encourage us, comfort us, unite us,
make our joy complete. Amen.

WRONGFUL DEATH

Death is part of the life cycle
You live
You die
You live again
But what's right about death
When has death by violence ever been right?

What is wrong?
Violent Crime
Robberies
Homicide
Committed by a man
The father of one's children
Does that make it right?

To ram the back of a car
For SWAT to swarm
30 bullets fired into a car
Since the initial target was wrong,
Does the death of the unintended make your action right?

Your target is in the passenger's seat
Yet the life murdered was in the driver's
With a now motherless 4-month-old
A 4-month-old child in the back seat
A witness to execution
That is wrongful
That ain't right

Monetary restitution
May be the court's solution
But it won't raise the dead
Return life of mother to child
Until the last breath
Ain't nothing right about
Wrongful Death

#India Kayger

ROBBING PETER

Black
Woman
Widow
Three strikes off the bat
Counting pennies
Counting nickels
Counting dimes
Utility bills
Mortgage
Drowning
How to do this?
What you doing here?
Grab shovel
Get off my property
Let me get to the store
Robbing Peter
Grab some money orders
At least get a minimum payment
$22.09 I think it is
Can hardly get home
Two more utility workers at my house
I'mma fix this right now
Go to kitchen
Grab a knife
These folks are going to get out my yard
Late or not
I'm trying to fix this
Done robbed Peter just to get what I need for the minimum

Now police showing up
Told to drop my knife
Threw it
Turned my back to go back in the house
12 shots fired
From 8 feet away
Lower body and legs
Fatal shot to the chest
Dead yet body handcuffed in the grass
Defiance is what you saw
Death for a black woman turning her back on the law
Just trying to survive
Robbing Peter to pay Paul

#Eula Mae Love

MORNING ANNOUNCEMENTS

These are your morning announcements.

Due to COVID-19, closures services will continue to be broadcast on our internet channel.

Those who may lack internet access and capability can contact the church office for support.

Our voter registration block party has gone virtual.

We have guest speakers, presentations, an exciting panel, and music performances by local artists.

The hospitality will still be providing food, so drive through and pick up your prepared meals.

For those participating in the marches, there will be a virtual session during our regular Bible Study to discuss Preparation for Demonstration.

For those who have been affected by COVID-19 through sickness, employment, etc., please let the ministry team know.

We have structures in place to help support specific identified needs.

Service, meeting, and program times have been modified.

To support and acknowledge family needs during this time

If you are participating in any of the on-campus outreach opportunities

Wear a mask, gloves, and plan for social distancing as we serve our community

For news and updates, go to the website and check the bulletin

Ministry of this house continues until we are able to meet again.

FAIL

Another Epic
Positively Epic
Notably Epic
Astoundingly Epic
Seriously Epic
Fail

Failure of equity
Failure of equality
Failure of civil rights
Failure of justice
Failure of health care
Fail

Accident
Vehicle Rollover
Not the call of an ambulance
Assessing needs for mental health
Not checking vitals to see if all was well
Police accusation of a controlled substance
Not accurately self-identifying to officer demands
Fail

Just flip it and reverse the story in your favor
Blame the victim for their health decline
Not taking responsibility for your job behavior
Complaining to the family of headaches and wanting to blackout
Supposedly seen by medical staff over loss of appetite

No accountability for the lack of care and medical response
In two weeks of incarceration and blood clots
Blame it on genetics, but to come to an actual conclusion, you cannot
Fail

This system failure shows the instability of the foundation
The systemic structures ingrained in the blood and policies of the
nation
How then can we claim to be the greatest
If we cannot provide our citizens with equal rights under the law
and equitable treatment?
And for this cause, another black woman dies
Because a system targeted against its people just can't get it right

Disastrous Fail
Fatal Fail
Habitual Fail
Epic Fail

#Symone Marshall

ON VIDEO

I know you saw it on video

Heard about it on radio

Local news gave it little attention
So, here's what the stories didn't mention

Four taser shots after handcuffed
Cuffed behind the back as if it wasn't enough
Shackled around the legs

A hobble strap to restraints
Then the nerve to a spit mask over the face

So, this is how law enforcement treats the mentally ill?
No knowledge, no understanding, just do as they will?
Investigating to check for any criminal violation
Declined to release video while under investigation

For a 5'3, 130 lb. woman, it seems so much extra
That you'd require 6 deputies to keep this woman together
So, a standard restraint wouldn't immobilize your hands
The worse possible scenario is what you have at hand
She could slip her hands through the restraint
Pulled belt up to her chest
Then with her hand free, be mobile enough to attack?

After being rushed to the hospital, homicide detectives were turned away
No answers from the victim while alive
Not allowed until death to truly investigate
Just another story of a black girl with mental issues not ending well
Video evidence remains the story to tell

Yet despite what you see on video as true
Being black with mental health issues can make you a hashtag too

#Natasha McKenna

OFFERING

What we have to offer is small considering what You O God have given to us.
You have given us the daily gift of life and the eternal life that comes through relationship.
All that we have comes from You.
We are grateful and thankful for the opportunity to give.
May we give with great joy in our hearts
Knowing that our giving
Supports Your work
Use us for Thy glory and service
Bless these gifts we offer today

A NEW RESPONSE

It's time for a new response
Time for answers
Time for action
Just time

Walked with a cane
Yet supposedly holding two knives
Just finished a phone argument with her girlfriend
Confronted by officers outside of her shelter
Just trying to re-enter a building
Making a lunge after officers
A refusal to follow a given direction
Back turned
14 fatal shots fired
This is how you address someone with a mental health condition?

It's time for a response
A different response
A comprehensive response
An empathetic response
A response that fits the needs
A change in structure and function response

With respect for life
A respect for space
Respect for one's being
Yvonne deserved that kind of response
57, black, disabled, homeless, and lesbian

These descriptors considered crimes
But she received what came naturally
The you are less than response

You are not worthy of response
You're a non-factor response
You don't submit to authority response
Automatic response of death

I need a response
We need a response
Not business as usual
A changed response
A humane response
Clear, solid, equitable
So, we can get a different result

#Yvonne McNeil

NO CHARGES

When a service is rendered, there is a charge
When making a purchase, there is a charge
From food, clothing, and shelter
To lights, heat, and water
They have a charge
Additional fees and a charge
April 15, the IRS expects full payment of its charge

Yet for the taking of a life
Especially if nonwhite, no charge?
I'm grilling outside in front of my home
What's really the problem here
'Cause I don't see one

To be threatened with a ticket
Then placed in a chokehold
A continuation of the violent behavior of police unfolds
This kind of behavior shouldn't be tolerated or condoned
Since when can't you grill in front or in the backyard of your own
home

It's like daily walking on pins and needles, living on guard
To constantly violate the rights of people of color and there never
is a charge

#Rosann Miller

HYMN OF PREPARATION: VIRTUOUS WOMAN
(AN INTERPRETATION OF PROVERBS 31:10-31)

Who can find a capable woman?
Her family knows they can trust in her
More valuable than a ruby or diamond.
They do not lack and with no need for fear
I'm committed to you for the rest of my life
Working with my hands
Will do you good no evil or strife
Let me help you understand

I am
I am
I am
A virtuous woman
Woman

Making sure my family is eating right
Consider some property in which to invest
Taking care of details sometimes into the night
I may be a boss, but I know self-care and rest
I advocate for resources and needs of the community
Not worried about home because I took care of that first
If I've got it to give, I'll do what I can to meet the need
'Cause when it comes to serving others, I don't just talk; I put in work
I am
I am

I am
A virtuous woman
Woman

My style speaks strength and demands respect
Walking and wisdom and speaking the ways of kindness
Not one to be idle; even just a little bit
I know and fear the Lord, and my family calls me blessed
The works I've done will speak for me
And a harvest in the time to come I will see

I am
I am
I am
A virtuous woman
Woman

SHOPPING CART

In my shopping cart is my life
My clothes, toiletries, the basics and whatnots
College-educated, had a banking career
Now widowed and homeless
All I have and own is in here
In this shopping cart

A shopping cart
A shopping cart
Police stop me for my shopping cart
Questioning if I stole the shopping cart
The grocery store ain't coming for me
Why can't I go about my business
And y'all let things be?

2 bicycle cops with nothing better to do
Than to harass a middle-aged black woman with mental issues
I just take my cart and keep moving the other way
Grab the screwdriver for protection; just leave me alone today
At 5'1, 100 pounds, the officers fell into a state of fear
In fear for their lives
So fatal shot fired is what you've got here
For a woman

A black woman
A middle-aged black woman
A middle-aged homeless black woman
A middle-aged homeless black woman with mental health issues

Not about a stolen vehicle
Not about stolen goods
But over a shopping cart
A life gone over a shopping cart

#Margaret Mitchell

EXCUSES

Excuses
How many can you devise?
How many can you come up with?
Do they just roll off the tongue as easily as a white lie?
Or with constant repetition, an action becomes justified?

Excuses
What does orientation have to do with it?
What does mental health status have to do with it?
Were you not trained in how to respond to a crisis?
Why do we keep circling back to this?

Excuses
To call someone "it?"
To call someone in a schizophrenic crisis "combative?"
What happened to decency and respect?
Obviously, there was no training for that

Excuses
To justify the use of excessive force
To blame the victim for the actions of police restraint
Neglect and vitals not checked in the context of custody
Another life silenced in death.

Excuses
Explanation offered
Reason for a fault
Used to justify the failure of a trust

A trust to protect and serve
Meaningless device
Can't keep rationalizing last breaths at the cop's hands

Tired of excuses
Don't need your excuses
You can keep your excuses
Done

#Kayla Moore

SERMON TITLE: BY THE HAND OF A WOMAN
SCRIPTURE TEXT: JUDGES 4:4-5:24

At the time of the text, Israel's children lived under great oppression.
Living in sin had become a pattern of on- and off-again relationship
with God.
So, as usual, this is how the story went.
They'd cry to the Lord, get a judge and, for a while, repent.
But this time, they cried a little louder than before.
So, God raised up a prophetess called Deborah.
She was married and judged the people for a length of time.
She'd been given a strategy to defeat Israel's enemies from the Divine.
It was Israel's military captain, Barak, whom she charged to go.
But he needed to be handheld, so Deborah upfront let him know.
Because he did not heed and follow the Lord's command.
The honor and victory would be by a woman's hand.
And when Sisera, leader of Israel's enemy forces, came into Jael's
tent,
He asked her for safety and water.
She covered him with a mantle and gave him milk.
When sleep fell upon him, with hammer and nail in hand,
She drove the nail into his temple, fastening him to the ground, and
he was dead.
Songs of praises would be sung of Jael's bravery throughout the
land.
God gave his people victory by a woman's hands, just as Deborah
had said.

WITHOUT DOCUMENTATION

Without documentation
There's no written record
What gets reported ends up based on remembrances and single
words
Details go missing
It becomes he said she said
Then you have a case like this where someone ends up dead

A trans woman of color receiving a courtesy ride from a bar
A simple trip from bar to home wasn't going to be far
So, in your wisdom and authority, you called off medics
Who would have better handled the situation
They would have taken her to the hospital for intoxication
Officers assured the bystanders and witnesses that she'd be taken to
a place of safety
Nizah was a far cry from where she would be only 64 hours later to
die from a head injury
Yet she wouldn't make it home that day
Officer basically drops her off three miles away
But the ride itself was not reported or documented
So, no one can be held accountable for what would follow then
Nizah's body is later found bleeding with a fractured skull
Noted as a hospital case and not a criminal one
A prompt investigation of her injury did not even occur
What we have of the 911 call by their officers is that she was a crime
victim
With only fragments of the report, files are mysteriously misplaced
Many are still missing from the city's archives even today

When you make a case, you have little to stand on
When nobody cared to note in the logs, and you have no documentation

Records do show how persons in the trans community
Are harassed and physically/sexually assaulted by the police
While a small settlement was reached by the family
For a community in mourning, where there's no justice, there's no peace

#Nizah Morris

BLAME THE WOMAN

If food was burned
Blame the woman
If the kids fail
Blame the woman
If a bill is late
Blame the woman
If the house ain't clean
Blame the woman
For all the issues in the world
It's just easy to blame the woman

You blame the woman
And you don't have responsibility
Blame the woman
There are no consequences, no accountability
If you blame the woman, you can go your own way
No matter the facts; no matter what was said

With all the expectations, how do you manage the stress?
Young and trying to figure out your own issues and mess
Don't have time to be the blunt of your blame
Trying to get my life together no time for games
I got into a heated argument with grandma, my fam
I took off in her car just needed time to figure out a plan
The car wasn't stolen, so why call the police
By now, that's just automatic endangerment
If you'd watch the news, you'd see
Officers claim I was driving erratically

Led them on a high-speed chase
Driving down the wrong way
Then ramming into a patrol car trying to get away
The passengers deny the claim they shot in self-defense
Nah, control of the car was lost, and she crashed
The shot was fired; that's how it went

This is not the way that this had to end
Just keep blaming the woman again and again

#Gabriella Nevarez

HYMN OF INVITATION
(TO THE TUNE OF I HAVE DECIDED)

I have decided to lift my sister
I have decided to lift my sister
I have decided to lift my sister
I've got your back
I've got your back

Violence behind me
Equality before me
Violence behind me
Equality before me
Violence behind me
Equality before me
I've got your back
I've got your back

If you're not with me
I'll still go forward
If you're not with me
I'll still go forward
If you're not with me
I'll still go forward
I've got you back
I've got your back

WHY SETTLE?

Why settle?
Some may ask or say
There was a crime committed
Someone should have to pay
At the end of the day, we all know what this is
Officers and their departments are shielded from financial
consequences

Why settle?
Bullying and silencing of victims and their families
From having their just say
Prevents accountability whether the department or police
It's the taxpayer that pays

Why settle?
Obvious lack of transparency and exposure
Over cities having to borrow
Given the number of incidents
What would the city have to borrow for?
Why settle?

Settle because
You can't be black and gathered in a group
Without something criminal going on
Not simple kicking with a few friends, talking smack and having fun
I was just walking on my way home
To get stopped by more than one
More than one officer to claim

They saw me put something in my mouth before they pursued
Didn't think it could have been candy or even gum that was being
chewed?

Settle because
Thrown to the grown, knee on the chest
"Spit it out" is what witnesses heard officers say
Officers said I had choked to death on 5 small bags of cocaine
Death by strangulation is what witnesses reported and saw
Neither officer attempted CPR or tied to revive me
And you want us to respect the law?

Settle because
Three young children are left without a mother
Who will meet their basic needs besides each other?
There was no cocaine or other drugs to be found in my system
Yet the Office of Professional Standards found no criminal
wrongdoing
Nobody gets charged, and life moves on
Settlement for the family but justice not yet won

#Frankie Ann Perkins

NOT AGAIN

Not again
Not again
Another young woman
Another black woman
Another young black woman
Found dead in a cell

With a charge of disorderly conduct
Resisting arrest
Outside a private party, she was attending with friends
6 officers involved in the arrest
To get answers, a family awaits a death certificate

She tried to get help
Mama was the first to be called
To tell that she'd been arrested
Handcuffed and body slammed against a police car
Before being thrown into the vehicle

Not again
Not again
Equity now
Equality now
Protection now
If not now, when?

Pepper sprayed
Young woman complained of not being able to breathe

She had asthma
She had a breathing problem
Not something that could be ignored
Or a case where treatment could have waited

Mom didn't have the money
She couldn't make the bail
So, until the appointed time, she'd have to remain in jail
Mother can't get autopsy report, video footage, or details
Getting the run around by government officials doesn't sit well

They said they decontaminated her from the pepper spray before putting her in the cell
Wouldn't it make sense, given her issues, to do a medical or tox screen as well?
You arrested her allegedly for disorderly conduct
Would you want proof of your report to substantiate your claim?

Yet here we go again
18-year-old black woman can't get a break
Victim because criminal
How much more can we take?

#Sheneque Proctor

CALL TO DISCIPLESHIP
Based on Micah 6:8

In this sacred place
As you occupy Holy space
We call your hearts to be open
Your spirits to receive
A most divine message that we are called to believe
To follow that which the Lord requires
No time for complaining or throwing in the towel
What the Lord requires is not a request, but a must-do
What does the Lord require of you?
To do the work of justice
To love goodwill
To walk in humility with God
As we honor the memory of those who have gone before
We dare not rest but continue the charge and pick up the mantle
We are moving forward
Is there one?
Will there be one?

SPECIAL

Thoughts come faster than I can speak
Sometimes 5 hours or less is when I sleep
I need to move, just can't be still
Just can't just sit and chill
I'm just wonderful and special, and that's not arrogance
Call overconfidence if you want
Could be called manic behavior by a psychiatrist
Special
I'm just special

So impulsive, maybe some at-risk behavior
A mother with a law degree, a son who I adored
Yet I have those times of being energetically engaged
Then spirally into disconnection
Sometimes things just don't feel the same
And just like moods, interest in activities may change
Special
I'm just special

Eating and sleeping habits can go to the extreme
Binging on junk food to basically not wanting to eat
Awake all night or days you can't get out of bed
It's something else trying to manage what's happening in my head
Special
I'm just special

What's going to happen to me when I die?
Reading obituaries becoming obsessed

Having thoughts of suicide
All of these are signs and symptoms of bipolar disorder
Something treated with meds and therapy
Not to be handled by police officers
Special
I'm just special

My daddy watched the video
He knew what was happening
Told the reporter of my bipolar disorder
He understood
An erratic driving spree
He loves me
He says I'm special
He said I was special

Cell phone video recorded the chase
Steered the cars toward officers
Life ending in a full bullet spray
There's got to be some changes to this whole policing structure
Nobody should have to die by police hands
Because of a mental disorder
Special
I was special

#Michelle Shirley

THE WRONG ONE

You've got the wrong one
You've got the wrong one
Not the right address
Not the right family or children
What you claim is going on couldn't have happened here
I told you, you got the wrong one
Can't you hear

Just getting out of the shower
When hearing a loud noise
A dozen police officers banging and surrounding at my door
Said that they had an allegation of a child being harmed
I told them that it wasn't this apartment and that they had the wrong
one
But with my response, the officers were not satisfied

You've got the wrong one
You've got the wrong one
Not the right address
Not the right family or children
What you claim is going on couldn't have happened here
I told you, you got the wrong one
Can't you hear

I was only wearing a towel dragging me half-naked to the hallway
outside
I use an oxygen tank
I'm dealing with chronic obstructive pulmonary disease

Having problems breathing
I need my inhaler
Someone help me, please

A neighbor captured the incident on video
As I collapsed to the floor
I was traumatized
Overcome with waves of embarrassment, more and more
The children were even brought out of the home
And dragged out into the hall
They even placed them in handcuffs
And they hadn't done anything wrong

You got the wrong one
You got the wrong one
Not the right address
Not the right family or children
What you claim is going on couldn't have happened here
I told you, you got the wrong one
Can't you hear?

Why would you cuff the children if you suspected abuse?
This is either a power trip or authority misuse
Physically exposed in the hallway video recording the incident
available for all to see
No regard for basic human rights or my dignity
Only for the officer to finally go to the correct apartment
And finally, put a towel over me

You got the wrong one
You got the wrong one

Not the right address
Not the right family or children
What you claim is going on couldn't have happened here
I told you, you got the wrong one
Can't you hear?

#Denise Stewart

RECESSIONAL: MAY THE LORD GOD BLESS YOU REAL GOOD
ARTIST: TWINKIE CLARK, ALBUM: THE MASTERPIECE

Chorus
"May the Lord, God bless you real good,
May the Lord, God bless you real good;
Woke me up this morning,
started me on my way
Let me see a dawning of a brand new day.
Real good (real good),
Real good (real good),
May the Lord,
May the Lord,
May the Lord, God, bless you real good

Verse
Be encouraged my sister my brother
He's got blessings in store above
May the Lord God bless you real good
I know the tempter tried to tempt you so,
(Hold on 'till He blesses you).

He's busy trying to keep the saints from reaching their goal,
(Hold on 'till He blesses you).
God has something good in store for you,
If you'll be faithful in everything you do.

Chorus

Bridge
Real good (real good),
Real good (real good),
May the Lord,
May the Lord,
May the Lord God bless you real good.

Vamp
May the Lord,
Bless you,
Bless you,
Bless you.

Ending
May the Lord God bless you real good."[3]

3. Clark, Twinkie The Masterpiece:May the Lord God Bless You Real Good. 1996.
Public Domain: https://www.elyrics.net/read/t/twinkie-clark-lyrics/may-the-lord-god-bless-you-real-good-lyrics.html Accessed 9/28/20

IN MY HOME

In my home
I go and come as I please
My name is on the lease
I pay the bills
I have the keys

In my home
The place I let my hair down and be
Finished working a shift for the man
I want to relax and just breathe

I can just be in the company of family and friends
Having a good time
Or Netflix and chill and a meal with my bae
I'm at home, and I'm fine

Can't put my finger on it, but something's a bit off
Hearing movement like footsteps yet soft
Let me just finish what I'm doing, eat, watch TV, call it a night
No knock, what the...?
Shots fired, like a war zone
Barging in, disrupting the peace of my home

My sacred space
Now entrance into the divine grace
Shots fired… one, two, three
In my home, but the search warrant wasn't for me
Shots fired… four, five, six

By the time the truth is told
The story will have a fabricated twist
Shots fired …seven, eight
Last gasp, then silence

Future dreams in plans in an instant gone
Can't even be safe in my own home

#Breonna Taylor

ANSWER ME THIS

They say there are more questions than answers, but…
Answer me this
How does a black woman end up on top of a hospital roof?
With her three-year-old son and a butcher knife?
So
Answer me this
You used pepper spray to subdue
So, wasn't that enough?
The child was released
You couldn't take her without the use of excessive force?
So
Answer me this
Why so many shots?
And why shots in the back?
In what world does lunging with the left make sense?
Especially for someone who is right-hand dominant?
So
Why continue firing?
Why keep firing?
Already down
Too many questions

I know there won't be no answers
Just another dirty cop cover-up
LAPD style
They've got a history
The blue ain't new to this
They true to protect and serve their own

Child left
Mother dead and gone

More questions than answers
Won't answer
Ain't trying to answer
Refuse to answer
Just a little of this question
A bit of this question
Some of these questions
Any of these questions
No not one
No answers for those wearing a shield and carrying the gun

#Sonji Taylor

CLOSING REMARKS

You have watched the news. You have read articles or blogs and listened to podcasts or reports on the radio. You have attended town hall meetings or participated in protests and marches. Is this enough? Is there more? Maybe you have done none of the above-mentioned things, and being so frustrated by what you have seen or heard around you have given up any hope of change and have become apathetic. The words found in Micah 6:8 then become a motivation for action. "He has told you, O mortal, what is good; and what does the LORD require of you but to do justice, and to love kindness, and to walk humbly with your God."

If you're unsure of what you can do, you can check out some suggestions from, The 5-Minute Advocate: "1. Define the issue, 2. Identify possible solutions, and 3. Develop an engagement plan."[4] Knowledge is power, so if you're talking about police brutality and reform, it is important to be aware of both sides of the issue. As you identify possible solutions, you can access public records and gather other pertinent data to support why your recommendation would be a plausible solution. None of this work can be accomplished alone, so having a team or a coalition of support is crucial.

Also, recognize that you don't have to reinvent the wheel. There may be several community organizations and programs that are addressing the issue that you are concerned about, and you can join them in their efforts. Your plan of engagement may include the following methods of communication with policymakers: organizing public forums, emails, or arranging face-to-face meetings. These are just a few ways of moving from apathetic to change catalyst, and in doing so, you live out the call of the stated Scripture to do what is right, love mercy, and walk with God in humility.

4.Johnson, Chonya. The 5 Minute Advocate: Get In! Get Out! & Get Results!. Chonya Johnson: Spring, Texas. 2012 Kindle Version Location 55 of 184,

JOB REQUIREMENTS

To be a police officer, you need a minimum of high school diploma
or GED
Doesn't quite match up with the depth of responsibilities
One to maintain law and order
That's part of the training
The reason they give you a gun for
A gun to be used for deterring crime
Yet too often used excessively on black and brown bodies time after
time

Responsible for protecting and serving people and their property
Evidently, that service applies to everybody but me
Investigating crimes and apprehending violators is the expected
norm
But somehow, the criminal justice system becomes a people's
revolving door
African Americans are less than 20% of the nation's population
Yet the numbers imprisoned far exceed that representation
To improve the quality of life of citizens
Just doesn't seem to work for the community I live in

All I did was drop off and leave my kids
I was on the brink of a breakdown, so that's what I did
Isn't leaving them at the fire department or the police station
considered a safe haven
Aren't you supposed to be able to leave them without judgment or
question?
But instead of help, I'm arrested for child endangerment

Trying to get a better life for my kids was my predicament

What am I supposed to do but resist?
I had committed no crime for you to arrest me like this
Reported handcuffing and restraints, but I was literally kicked in the groin
I'm sure that is not appropriate protocol given the situation
Complaints of pain and inability to breathe were ignored
Until I appeared lifeless in the back of the patrol car
Call made to the paramedics, but it was too little too late
To succumb to police brutality seals this young black mother's fate.

#Alesia Thomas

RIDE OR DIE

To ride is an option
To die is an inevitable truth to be determined
It's giving consent
To be attached to
To be a part of
When you make a decision
A decision to ride or die

But when does the ride or die
Become ride and die?
When is the option lost?
At what point did I lose the agency to choose?
'Cause I'm black?
'Cause I'm homeless?
'Cause a black male and a black female together?
'Cause we're together in a car?
Two people can't be together driving in a car?
No matter how raggedy but together?

So the car backfires
Sounding like a gunshot, so that gives reason to give chase
Can only imagine the amount of fear and adrenaline felt that day
High speeds hitting one hundred
Mr. Officer, how you see a firearm in the car driving that fast?
You the one chasing

One cop opens fire
Then another

They all join in the fray
Bullets just flying
137 shots fired
Bloodied bodies pulled from the car
No assessment of the situation
Just excuses

Scared for my life
Unarmed couple on the inside
Bad and bold to stand on top of the car
Fire into the windshield
Yet you're the one afraid
Suspension for violations
Acquittal of manslaughter charges
To have jobs reinstated

Black man and a black woman
Together, they take a ride
Failure to pull over for a turn signal violation became a chase to ride
and die
Only in this life in black bodysuits
You become target
Ride and Die

#Malissa Williams

BENEDICTION

(A REINTERPRETATION OF JUDE 1:24)

Now unto God, our Creator who is able to keep you from dying
Now unto God, the Righteous Judge to whom vengeance belongs, and it will be paid
Now unto the all-knowing One, our God who hears our righteous cause
Now unto God before whom we boldly stand without fault, without blame
But with exceeding joy be glory, majesty, and power
Amen.

CHALLENGE

We realize that life has its ups and downs
We don't always have the words
We keep forward movement, often forcing an outside smile on an inward frown
Without thinking of harmful effects or personal damage
We skip the humanity, and the person or situation becomes a challenge

Why you all up on me?
I said I didn't need any help
I was just looking at these shades
Why you want to make it into something else?
Jumped in the car to get away from a disturbance at the mall
Got chased by a police officer to be shot 5 times in all
An officer in front of me, an officer behind me
Who could help but feel overwhelmed and trapped?

My family will speak for me and say that I was unarmed
Officers will declare they feared for their lives, and my vehicle was the weapon
While the medical examiner will rule it a homicide
Pushback would be inevitable as officers narrated their side
For going off or cursing an officer
Why didn't you let it be?
Between officers and witnesses, there are a lot of conflicting stories

It's a shame that as a result of fear, you can only manage
To view someone black and unarmed as a threat and a challenge

#Janet Wilson

NOT YOUR SHIELD

The body of the black woman continues to be brutalized
We skip childhood innocence and are immediately sexualized
Not allowed to be soft or need to seek protection
Our stereotype becomes angry and aggressive
We dare to dream of better days, circumstances, a better life
We hold fast to dreams, unwilling to let them die
Often shedding the same tears our mothers cried
Where can a sister find safety?
Tell me if you will
That I may not constantly be sacrificed
Become a human shield

Yet over and over again, we become the one
The sacrificial lamb, while internally become undone
Too much anxiety, too much stress
But a colored girl has to keep pushing and can't rely on getting help
Trying to juggle and take care of just the basic needs
Where's the time for self-care and soul healing
Where can a sister find safety?
Tell me if you will
That I may not constantly be sacrificed
Become a human shield

When you're pregnant, you're going through some changes
Weight gain, hormonal shifts, and picking up strange eating habits
Preparing for a newborn, you can lose focus
Not realizing relationship and environment shifts and not asking the
important questions

Like why has a SWAT team broken into the bedroom of our home?
That you and your father were under investigation for some recent shootings
I'm resting on my side in the bed, but you, who I love, turned and used my body as a shield
So you can keep dodging deputies' bullets and fire back at will

Finding myself in the crossfire
An innocent bystander, pregnant and tired
My boyfriend was the intended target suspected of crimes related to drugs
Claims there wasn't an announcement, so how do you explain what the situation was?
An unarmed black woman sacrificed, and by deputies, a collateral damage kill
You live to breathe another day despite a not guilty plea
Only because you used me as a shield

Not thinking of the two lives your actions cost
That provide and protect was a total loss
Where can a sister find safety?
Tell me if you will
That I may not constantly be sacrificed
Become a human shield.

#Alteria Woods

POSTLUDE

"Amen, Amen
Amen, Amen, Amen."

BIBLIOGRAPHY

-Clark, T. (1996). elyrics. Retrieved from elyrics.net: https://www.elyrics.net/read/t/twinkie-clark-lyrics/may-the-lord-god-bless-you-real-good-lyrics.html. Accessed September 28, 2020.

-Dharmaraj, G. E. (2020, April 27). National Council of Churches-National of Council of Churches of Christ in the USA. Retrieved from nationalcouncilof churches.us: https://nationalcouncilofhcurches.us/an-affirmation-of-faith/ Accessed September 27, 2020.

-Hairston, J. (1964). Jesster-Hairston-amen-lyrics. Retrieved from Genius.com: https://genius.com/Jester-hairston-amen-lyrics Accessed September 28, 2020.

-Weldon, J. W. (1921). Teaching Tolerance. Retrieved from tolerance.org: https://www.tolerance.org/classroom-resources/texts/lift-every-voice-and-sing#:~:text=This%20text%20is%20in%20the,or%20the%20Black%20National%20Anthem.&text=%E2%80%9CLift%20Every%20Voice%20and%20Sing%E2%80%9D%20was%20first%20a%20poem%20and,a%20hymn%20set%. Accessed September 27, 2020.

Made in the USA
Middletown, DE
01 June 2023

31544515R00066